Fir

By Beth Sycamore

Contents

CELEBRATION PRESS
Pearson Learning Group

A Very Famous Address

Can you imagine what it would be like to grow up in the White House? The White House is where the President of the United States works and lives. His family, the First Family, lives there too.

The President and his family live at
1600 Pennsylvania Avenue in Washington, D.C.

During the past 200 years, about 190 "first kids" have called 1600 Pennsylvania Avenue in Washington, D.C. home. In addition to Presidents' children, many nephews, nieces, and grandchildren of Presidents also lived at and visited the White House.

White House Firsts

1800 Susanna Adams, granddaughter of President John Adams, first child to live at the White House

1806 James Madison Randolph, grandson of President Thomas Jefferson, first child born at the White House

1893 Esther Cleveland, daughter of President Grover Cleveland, first President's child born at the White House

Living at the White House is very exciting. After all, how many kids get to meet a king or sit next to a princess? Susan Ford, daughter of President Gerald R. Ford, thought it was like "living a fairy tale," but

President Gerald R. Ford
★ 1974-1977 ★

for others it's like living in a fish bowl. It is hard to be in the spotlight all of the time.

3

About the White House

In 1792 a contest was held to find the best plan to build a special house for the President. Nine plans were sent in, and James Hoban's plan won.

On November 1, 1800, John Adams, the second President, moved into the new house. It

President John Adams ★ 1797-1801 ★

was very cold and damp. Only six rooms were finished. Because the grounds were muddy, the First Family had to walk across a wooden bridge to get to the front door.

Many changes have since been made to the White House. Porches, offices, and rooms have been added to make it more useful for the President and his family, the staff, and visitors. Today the White House is a grand mansion with four floors, and 132 rooms.

A cutaway of the White House

By the Numbers

- 132 rooms
- 35 bathrooms
- 28 fireplaces
- 8 staircases
- 3 elevators
- 1 swimming pool
- 1 movie theater
- 1 bowling alley
- 1 tennis court

Every new First Family makes changes to the White House to make it feel more like home. Some families bring their own furniture. Others use the furniture that is passed down from one President to the next. Some First Families have had special things built, such as a swimming pool, a bowling alley, and a movie theater.

Only the First Family and their guests can go to the family **quarters** on the second floor. There are many rooms there, including a sitting room and an office.

Some first kids discovered hidden places. Patti Davis, President Ronald Reagan's daughter, found a hidden **passage**. "I spent a little bit of time sitting in the stairwell in this little secret passageway. It was sort of a great escape."

President Ronald Reagan
★ **1981-1989** ★

Chelsea Clinton watches the Super Bowl with her dad, and the former governors of Texas and New York, at the White House family theater.

About 100 people help with housework at the White House. Like you, most first kids have to clean up their own messes. Chelsea

President William J. Clinton ★1993-2001★

Clinton had to sweep up the popcorn after watching movies in the White House theater.

When Dad Works at Home

The President works in a large room in the White House called the **Oval Office**. There he meets with his staff and special guests from around the world. Sometimes a first kid plays there, too, as John Kennedy Jr. did.

President John F. Kennedy ★ 1961-1963 ★

President Kennedy's son, John Jr., played under the desk in the Oval Office while his father met with his staff.

Tad Lincoln painted a mustache on this photo of himself dressed up as a soldier.

Some first kids find it hard to share their dad. Tad and Willie, young sons of President Abraham Lincoln, liked to play war games in the White House. Once when the President was in a very important meeting, Tad shot toy cannonballs at the door.

President Abraham Lincoln
★ **1861-1865** ★

Of course, every President tries to make time for his children. Afternoons at four o'clock were the "children's hour" for the Roosevelt family. During this time President Theodore Roosevelt would read from his favorite book or tell stories about his exciting cowboy adventures.

President Theodore Roosevelt
★ **1901-1909** ★

President Kennedy's children were very young when they moved into the White House. John and Caroline spent lots of time with their dad. When John was able to walk, he thought his dad's desk was the perfect fort. It was a large desk made from the wood of an old ship. "And I just remember the inside that you could climb around in," said John years later. Sometimes his dad would reach under the desk to hand him a special treat.

Caroline Kennedy walks with her dad, President John F. Kennedy, on St. Patrick's Day.

Caroline Kennedy had breakfast dates with her dad. Sometimes he took her to special breakfast meetings. She would ride alongside her dad on her tricycle. When he told her it was time to go, Caroline would wave goodbye and pedal down the hall.

Meeting Special People

Important visitors from all over the world come to the White House for meetings, dinners, and parties. First kids must learn how to behave when they meet special guests.

Amy Carter meets the president of Mexico with her dad, President Jimmy Carter.

Chelsea Clinton met the 2000 U.S. Olympic athletes.

Over the years first kids have had the chance to shake hands with world leaders, movie stars, and famous **athletes**. Chelsea Clinton enjoyed talking with the U.S. Olympic team and had her picture taken with them.

School Time

If you're the President's son or daughter, you'll surely be watched in any school. Many first kids go to schools close to the White House. In the 1800s they traveled by horse and buggy. Today they ride in special bulletproof cars with **Secret Service** men tagging along.

Amy Carter was nine years old when she moved into the White House. She went to a public school just a few blocks away.

President Jimmy Carter ★ 1977-1981 ★

Chelsea Clinton went to a private school. Secret Service agents protecting her did not go into the classroom with her but watched from outside it. During her soccer games, they would sit in the bleachers to keep an eye on her.

Caroline Kennedy in the White House classroom

Caroline Kennedy didn't leave the White House to go to school. She just ran to the third floor. Mrs. Kennedy set up a special school there for her and about 20 friends. Sometimes they had to be quiet so they wouldn't disturb the President.

A Great Playground!

For many children the White House is the best playground around. "There's lots of room to play and a great big garden, too," said Caroline Kennedy after moving into the White House.

Quentin and Archie Roosevelt used to slide down the long staircases on large trays, which they borrowed from the kitchen. The Roosevelt family loved to play hide and seek. Even the President joined the fun.

President James Garfield's sons, Irvin and Abram, had pillow fights at the White House. Ann and David Eisenhower, grandchildren of President

**President
James A. Garfiel
★ 1881 ★**

**President
Dwight D. Eisenho
★ 1953-1961 ★**

Dwight D. Eisenhower, drove their tricycles up and down the White House driveway.

David and Ann Eisenhower ride their tricycles at the White House.

Some first kids liked quieter activities. Jesse Grant, son of President Ulysses Grant, watched the stars from the

President Ulysses S. Grant
★ 1869-1877 ★

White House roof with his telescope. Many years later Amy Carter enjoyed looking through a telescope at the night sky from the same roof.

Caroline Kennedy pushes her brother John on the swings.

In the White House yard, John and Caroline Kennedy had a treehouse, swing set, and **trampoline** near their father's office. Amy Carter also had a treehouse in a cedar tree that couldn't be seen from the street. She went there when she wanted to be alone.

Some first kids celebrate special days at the White House. Classmates surprised Amy Carter on her tenth birthday. They had a party and watched a movie in the White House theater. Everyone decorated pumpkins, even her dad, President Carter!

The cake at Amy Carter's surprise birthday party was shaped like a jack-o'-lantern.

First Kids and Their Pets

Dogs of all kinds have made the White House their home. Some chased squirrels or ducks across the lawn. Others sat on the White House steps waiting to greet special guests. Many just tagged along next to their masters.

Susan Ford and her family kept an eye on Liberty and her eight pups.

Quentin Roosevelt snuck his brother's pony, Algonquin, into the White House.

President Theodore Roosevelt's family had a small zoo at the White House. Once when Archie Roosevelt was very sick, his brother brought Archie's pony up the elevator to his room to cheer him up. Can you imagine a pony in the White House?

Roosevelt Family Pets

- bear
- lizard
- guinea pigs
- badger
- blue macaw
- rabbit
- dogs
- snakes
- one-legged rooster
- hyena
- barn owl
- raccoons
- kangaroo rats
- flying squirrel
- horned toad
- cats
- ponies
- horses

Chelsea Clinton's cat, Socks, in the White House

Photographers loved taking pictures of Socks, the black and white cat Chelsea Clinton brought with her to the White House. Socks had to learn quickly, though, how to share the spotlight with President Clinton and his dog, Buddy.

Life changes for the President's children when they move into the White House. Simple things like sleeping over at a friend's house become a big deal. Yet all of these children get to see history in the making. It's an adventure they'll never forget.

Twin daughters Barbara (far left) and Jenna Bush pose with President George W. and First Lady Laura Bush.

Glossary

athlete   a person who is skilled at games or sports

mansion   a very large, stately house

Oval Office   the room in the West Wing of the White House where the President works

passage   a way to pass through a place, such as a hall

quarters   a place where people live

Secret Service   the part of the government whose job is to guard the President and his family

spotlight   the attention or notice of the public

staff   a group of people who work for a company or organization

trampoline   a piece of canvas or rubber stretched on a frame that people can bounce on